The
Heart
of
Man

Andrew Wommack

Published in partnership between Andrew Wommack Ministries and Harrison House Publishers.

Woodland Park, CO 80863 – Shippensburg, PA 17257

ISBN 13 TP: 978-1-59548-724-7

ISBN 13 eBook: 978-1-6675-0981-5

For Worldwide Distribution.

1 2 3 4 5 6 / 27 26 25 24

Contents

Introduction

It seems like we talk about the heart all the time. As a matter of fact, the word *heart* is used 830 times in the *King James Version* of the Bible, in 762 verses.[1] Obviously, we aren't talking about your blood pump—your physical heart—but rather the core of who you are.

Are you seeking a better relationship with God? Do you want to serve the Lord, but believe something is holding you back? Do you want to live a holy life, but feel like you just can't change old behaviors?

As your heart goes, so goes your life. Many people try to change things in their life without changing their heart. This is just behavior modification. People try to change their actions but not what caused them. As a society, we do this same thing.

We want to get people to change and do things differently, but many people think it requires more education or some sort of government program. This kind of thinking says if we just give people more money, we could get them out of poverty. Basically, the world believes that we can somehow reach utopia if we just remove all the obstacles. They look at changing physical things to solve problems. But that is not what the Word of God teaches.

For as he thinketh in his heart, so is *he.*

Proverbs 23:7a

The Bible says that the way your heart goes is the way that your life goes. Your life is the way it is, not because of outside circumstances, but because of what you believe in your heart.

If we could somehow magically give everyone all the money they need, good jobs, good living conditions, health care, and whatever else they want, it would only be a matter of time until things go back to the way they are. Without changing the heart, life won't change. We are as we think in our hearts (Prov. 23:7).

Keep Your Heart

Keep thy heart with all diligence; for out of it are *the issues of life.*

Proverbs 4:23

This scripture tells us that we have the responsibility of keeping—or protecting—our hearts. You have to be diligent in protecting your heart because the issues of life proceed out of it. Your life actually comes out of your heart. Before you can learn how to protect your heart, you first have to know what your heart is. This is really important.

It has been generally understood that the words *heart* and *spirit* are interchangeable. But, as we'll see, that isn't always the case. To better understand this concept, we should first find out who we really are and how God made us to be.

And the very God of peace sanctify you wholly; and I pray God your whole spirit and soul and body be preserved blameless unto the coming of our Lord Jesus Christ.

1 Thessalonians 5:23

In other words, the Apostle Paul is saying, "I pray that God would sanctify your entire person," and then he said, "spirit, soul, and body." This is one of the clearest references in Scripture that we are three-part beings.

It's obvious that you have a physical body, but your spirit cannot be perceived by your physical senses (John 3:6). Therefore, the "natural man" (1 Cor. 2:14) cannot understand the existence and function of the spirit.

Likewise, it is easy to understand you have an inner part that the Bible refers to as the soul. This is what many call the personality. It is comprised of the carnal intellect, the emotions, the will, and the conscience. Many people use the terms *spirit* and *soul* interchangeably, but Paul made a clear distinction between them in the above verse from 1 Thessalonians.

Spirit, soul, and body— that's all that you've got! There isn't a separate part of you called the heart. But when we're talking about the term *heart*, we need to understand it in a biblical sense. The *heart* refers to the center of a person, where your life proceeds from.

You see, we cannot consistently operate differently than what we believe in our hearts. For example, when people lie to gain an advantage, their hearts control their actions. Our dominant actions are a window into our hearts. And if we want to change our actions, we have to change our hearts first. Anything less is just behavior modification and not true change.

Before we go deeper into discussing what the heart is, let's look at what the Bible has to say about the spirit and the soul, how they are different, and how they relate to one another. It really begins with your nature. You need to be born again before you can really see any change in your heart.

Sin Consciousness

For all have sinned, and come short of the glory of God.

Romans 3:23

When I was a kid, I used to have a dream that I smoked a cigarette, got caught, got turned in to the police, and then the police turned me over to my mother—which was worse! After my mother had nearly beaten me to death, I wound up in hell.

Every time I had this dream, I would wake up in a cold sweat. I had this same dream at least once or twice a year for probably five or six years. You may be thinking,

Boy, you were messed up. Well, I was! I was raised in a very legalistic environment.

As a child, in my early years of religious training, I was taught to write sin lists. Church leaders would give me and the other children paper, and we had to list every sin we'd ever committed. I typically had to ask for another piece of paper! They must have thought that if people saw how rotten they were, they would get sick of themselves and turn to God. But that's never the way it worked.

By making my sin list, I got so sick of myself that all I could think about was me. I didn't have time for God because I was so occupied with how much I had failed. When I would go into restaurants and see dirty words scribbled on the bathroom walls, I would leave there feeling totally guilty, condemned, and defiled. It took me days—weeks sometimes—to get over my exposure to that kind of stuff. Like the dream I had about smoking a cigarette, these experiences resulted in me feeling condemned.

I ended up being obsessed with sin instead of being focused on Jesus. People who weren't brought up in strict religious environments under condemnation may have trouble relating to that, but I am living proof that being sin-focused is a waste of time and energy.

Now, I don't believe smoking a cigarette will send a person to hell, but you will smell like you've already been there! The point I'm making is that the Law put such a fear in me that I never said a word of profanity, never took a drink of liquor, never smoked a cigarette, and never even tasted coffee. Some people may think, *Coffee?* Well, you've actually got a scripture to stand on for drinking coffee. Mark 16:18 says you can drink any deadly thing and it shall not harm you!

That may be funny, but I'm just saying that I've lived a holier life than most people have even thought about living. Nevertheless, it doesn't matter how good you are living if you are still headed to hell. It doesn't matter if you're a good sinner or a bad sinner. Who wants to be the best sinner who ever went to hell? Not me, amen! So, what I'm saying is, the Law can restrain the amount of sin you commit, but it still can't change your nature.

Are People Basically Good?

But to him that worketh not, but believeth on him that justifieth the ungodly, his faith is counted for righteousness.

Romans 4:5

A few years ago, Christian researcher George Barna released the results of a survey showing that nearly seven out of ten Americans view people as "basically good." This just goes against Scripture. But, sad to say, most people don't let the Bible get in the way of what they believe.

Even the Church does not understand these things. According to the survey, 70 percent of Evangelicals and Pentecostals agreed that "people are basically good."[2] I believe that kind of thinking is one of the reasons many Christians don't share their faith with other people.

People like their neighbors. They believe they're relatively good people, and they just think, *Well, they must be okay. Certainly they're going to make it, because good people are going to make it.* That's just wrong!

Jesus came to save sinners (1 Tim. 1:15). Unless people acknowledge that they are sinners, they cannot be saved. The Bible says, "*all have sinned, and come short of the glory of God*" (Rom. 3:23), and God only justifies the ungodly (Rom. 4:5). Therefore, until people come to the end of themselves and admit they are ungodly, they cannot be saved! So, if you think people are basically good, in a sense you are rejecting the Gospel for them.

Before the Lord really touched my life on March 23, 1968, I was living like a modern-day Pharisee. I was born again at eight years old, and I knew something had changed inside of me, but I didn't get a true revelation of God until I was eighteen years old. During that time, I heard in church that to continually please the Lord, I had to live a holy life, do all the right things, and avoid all the wrong things. I swallowed that doctrine hook, line, and sinker.

I became a human doing instead of a human being. I was doing anything and everything they told me to do. Although I was an introvert, during my teenage years, I went out witnessing on the normal Thursday night visitations and even started a special Tuesday night youth visitation. I was petrified of speaking to people, but I was even more afraid that the Lord wouldn't love me or answer my prayers if I didn't witness to others.

That kind of thinking came to an end the night the Lord rang my bell. I was at a youth group meeting on a Saturday night in the pastor's study at our church. I won't go into all the details, but the Lord showed up in a powerful way. As I said earlier, I was born again at a young age and lived a very holy life, but that night I saw my relative unworthiness in the face of God's true holiness, and I came up way short.

The Heart Is the Issue

Woe unto you, scribes and Pharisees, hypocrites! for ye make clean the outside of the cup and of the platter, but within they are full of extortion and excess. Thou *blind Pharisee, cleanse first that* which is *within the cup and platter, that the outside of them may be clean also.*

Matthew 23:25–26

In the wake of that experience, I turned myself inside out and began confessing every sin I ever committed—or even thought about committing. The Lord had shown me my hypocrisy and self-righteousness; that all my good works were like filthy rags in His sight (Is. 64:6). After an hour and a half of repenting, I waited to see what the Lord's response would be. To my surprise, instead of rejection, the supernatural love of God just overwhelmed me.

For more than four months, I was caught up in the love of God. I knew that God loved me, and for the first time in my life I knew it had nothing to do with my performance. He loved me because He was love, not because I was lovely. I ended up going out and witnessing to more people about Jesus because I had experienced the love of God than I ever did out of obligation or fear.

The mistake of thinking that doing right makes us right is the same error the Pharisees made. Religion has always preached that if we clean up our actions, our hearts will become clean too. Jesus taught just the opposite (Matt. 23:25–26). It's through a changed heart that our actions change. The heart is the issue. Actions are only an indication of what is in our hearts. Actions are the fruit the heart produces.

God looks on the heart—not the actions (1 Sam. 16:7). Of course, God sees our actions and will deal with us about them, but only because they are inseparably linked to our hearts (Prov. 23:7). It's our hearts that really concern God.

God loves you completely, separate from your performance. That's what the Bible calls grace. What you do affects you and others, but it doesn't affect God's love for you. Living a holy life will help you love God more, but it won't make God love you more. He loves you because you have accepted Jesus and what He did for you. That's truly good news!

You Need a New Heart

The heart is *deceitful above all* things, *and desperately wicked: who can know it?*

Jeremiah 17:9

America's Founding Fathers considered this scripture from Jeremiah when they were drafting the U.S. *Constitution*. Because unsaved people have a sin nature and their hearts are "desperately wicked," serving in a position of authority may corrupt them.

Our Founders set up the government as a constitutional republic (Ex. 18:21) with separation of powers (Is. 33:22), so no one person or group of people could become too powerful. John Adams, a Founding Father and second president of the United States, once wrote, "Our Constitution was made only for a moral and religious People. It is wholly inadequate to the government of any other."[3]

Some people think that if you just get around a campfire and sing, "Kumbaya," everybody's going to love each other. That's not what the Word of God teaches. The Bible teaches that people are wicked at their core. People have a sinful nature. This is the reason you must be born again—you have to get a new nature.

A person doesn't have to take a baby and teach them how to be bad. A child will be selfish, lie, steal, and do all kinds of things. They are born in sin. In Psalm 51:5, David said,

Behold, I was shapen in iniquity; and in sin did my mother conceive me.

This isn't talking about being born out of wedlock. This is talking about how David was born with a sin nature. You may not like to think about things this way, but you have to realize that you were born with a sin nature, I was born with a sin nature, and even a seemingly innocent little baby was born with a sin nature.

John Wesley commented on this verse, "This filthy stream leads me to a corrupt fountain: and upon a review of my heart, I find, that this heinous crime, was the proper fruit of my vile nature."[4] It is not our individual actions that pollute us. We were born polluted and pollute the waters more as we progress through life if we are not born again.

If people understood this, it would eliminate so much confusion. Some people think, *Well, I'm basically good and all I need is just a little bit of help*, and they come to the Lord with that kind of attitude. That's just wrong.

Salvation Is Available

But God commendeth his love toward us, in that, while we were yet sinners, Christ died for us.

Romans 5:8

One time, I went and spoke at a place in Okefenokee Swamp in Florida where there is a rehabilitation camp that takes in ex-convicts after they've served time. This place is surrounded by a swamp that is full of alligators. They had about 600 men there who were rapists, murderers, con artists, and things like that.

Now, most people who live a holy lifestyle would see a gulf between themselves and a bunch of ex-cons. They might think, *How am I ever going to minister to these people?* Well, I just went into that place and shared my testimony. I told them I've never said a word of profanity, never drank alcohol, never smoked a cigarette, or anything like that.

When I was done sharing my testimony with these men, I said, "There's not a person in here that is going to a worse hell than I would have gone to. We all are in the same boat!" And I began to preach grace unto them. That message really ministered to those men, and they received it. It had such an impact that, after I left, the man who ran that facility required everyone who came in to listen to that message. That's awesome!

If you think it's your individual sins that make you disconnected from God and worthy of judgment, then you're going to see your own sin as worse than somebody else's.

You may get into condemnation and start thinking, *How could God ever use me?* But once you understand that we "*all have sinned, and come short of the glory of God*" (Rom. 3:23), it doesn't matter what you've done.

You were a sinner, not because of individual actions, but because of your old sin nature. Jesus died and paid for your sins just as much as He paid for the sins of everybody else. Once people understand this, it opens salvation to everybody. It doesn't matter what they've done.

Jesus didn't come to save the godly. Romans 4:5 says that Jesus came to save the ungodly. Unless you're ungodly, you can't be saved. Anybody who thinks, *God, I've been living a holy life, and I know you're going to save me because of that*, can't be saved.

You've got to come to the end of yourself. You've got to come to a place where you realize you can't save yourself because you are not worthy to stand in the presence of God. You have to humble yourself and receive salvation as a gift.

Without Jesus, each of us would be a zero with the rim knocked off. A person plus Jesus equals nothing, but nothing plus Jesus equals everything. Before salvation, we were all dead in trespasses and sins.

Children of Disobedience

And you hath he quickened, *who were dead in trespasses and sins; wherein in time past ye walked according to the course of this world, according to the prince of the power of the air, the spirit that now worketh in the children of disobedience.*

Ephesians 2:1–2

When people die, they lose communication with people who are alive. There is a separation. Just as there is separation of the spirit from the body in physical death (James 2:26), a separation occurred between God and man in spiritual death.

God told Adam and Eve that in the day they ate of the forbidden fruit, they would surely die (Gen. 2:17). They didn't die physically that day, but they died spiritually. Man was no longer able to fellowship with God after the fall. There was a loss of spiritual life (Eph. 4:18) and communion with God.

This death took place in the spirit and resulted in death being passed on to the soul and physical body. The "dead" human spirit of an unsaved person still functions; it just functions independently of God. As the Apostle Paul explained in Ephesians 2:3, the lost human spirit actually became united to Satan so that people were "by nature the children of wrath."

As a result of spiritual death, mankind began to walk opposite of the ways that God had intended. It didn't happen all at once; it was a step-by-step departure. People are bound by habits and desires that they just can't break on their own. It is the nature of unsaved people to live in sin. The spirit that is united with the dead human spirit works disobedience in people.

I remember hearing a story about a little boy in church who was more interested in playing with his toy car than listening to the sermon. While the pastor was trying to preach, this little boy was standing up in the front of the room, running his toy car up and down the pew, and making "vroom, vroom," noises. It was a distraction!

Finally, the pastor got frustrated and shouted, "Stop it!" The little boy brought his little car to a screeching halt, and the pastor told the boy, "I want you to sit down and be quiet!" That little boy crossed his arms, planted himself in that pew, and said under his breath, "I may be sitting on the outside, but I'm standing up on the inside!"

That's a funny story, but I believe it illustrates something really important. Obedience can be demanded. It can be coerced. But submission is an attitude of the heart. There's just something inside a person that when God says, "Thou shalt not," they say under their breath, "Bless God, I shall!" That's the sin nature. And it's something we're all born with.

Don't Be a Housebroken Sinner

Wherefore, as by one man sin entered into the world, and death by sin; and so death passed upon all men, for that all have sinned.

Romans 5:12

The fact that people inherited their sin nature is a totally new concept to many Christians. Most people believe that it's what they do that makes them sinners. But this verse clearly teaches that sin entered the earth through one man, Adam, and that death is a result of that sin (Rom. 5:15). It's not our individual actions of sin that separate us from God. It's that sin nature.

Our sins don't make us sinners. We were born sinners, and we sin because that is our nature. The Apostle Paul said in Ephesians 2:3 that we "*were by nature the children of wrath.*" This is why Jesus said we "*must be born again*" (John 3:7). We received our sinful nature through our natural birth, and we only receive a new nature through a spiritual rebirth (John 3:6–7).

Over the years, I've noticed that some people treat their dogs like they are human beings. They clean them up, paint their toenails, and put bows in their fur. Some of you may have those kinds of dogs, and I'm not against you. But when I go over to people's houses, their dogs will sometimes come up and stick their noses in places that they shouldn't be. Then their owners get embarrassed, and say, "Oh, I'm so sorry they did that!" But I always tell them, "Hey, it's just the dog nature in them."

People have tried to train dogs to abide by human standards. They housetrain them, teach them to beg and pray, and do all kinds of human things. But a dog's nature is still that of a dog. That's why they will lick themselves, relieve themselves on the carpet, and do many things that their owners don't want them to do. That's their nature. If left to themselves, they act like dogs, because they are dogs.

You can get shampooed, learn to do tricks, and look good on the outside, but if you have not been born again, you are just a housebroken sinner. Your nature hasn't changed. You will still go to hell because that's where sinners go. But the person who accepts what Jesus did for them and puts their faith in Him gets a new nature and goes to heaven after death. That's where the ones with the new, righteous nature go. It all depends on which nature you have.

Every one of us was born with a sin nature and we have to be changed. That's why we need to be truly born again. God gives us a new spirit, and that begins to change everything.

The Born-Again Spirit

Therefore if any man be in Christ, he is a new creature: old things are passed away; behold, all things are become new. And all things are of God, who hath reconciled us to himself by Jesus Christ, and hath given to us the ministry of reconciliation.

2 Corinthians 5:17–18

It's true that we were all born sinners (Ps. 51:5) and had the nature of the devil working in us (Eph. 2:2–3). But when you come to Christ and receive salvation, you become a new creature.

Now, this isn't talking about your body. Your body didn't change. And your soul, which is what the Bible calls the mental-emotional part of you, didn't automatically change either, though it is subject to change. It is your spirit that is born again and made perfect (Heb. 12:22–23)!

At salvation, you become a brand-new creation. It didn't say you are becoming; it says you have become. All things are passed away; not are passing away. They have already passed away. And all things are of God.

Now, that shows something that is already complete. Your body will be redeemed (Rom. 8:18–25), and your mind can be renewed (Rom. 12:2), but it was your spirit that was reborn—it was totally changed at salvation. You received the same spirit that you will have throughout all eternity. It will not have to be changed or cleansed again. It has been sealed with the Holy Spirit (Eph. 1:13). It is sanctified and perfected forever (Heb. 10:10–14).

When I started to see these things in the Word of God, it radically transformed my life. I learned that God is a Spirit and He deals with me on the basis of who I am in the spirit (John 4:24). Because of that, I can worship God based on who I am in the spirit and not on how I act or feel in the flesh. In my born-again spirit, I'm totally righteous and holy (Eph. 4:24). That's awesome!

I know this may come as a complete shock to many of you, but there isn't an old sin nature left in you once you get born again. Most Christians have been taught to believe that after salvation, they are still the same at their core, and they live the rest of their lives trying to restrain that old sin nature. They believe they have two natures. That's schizophrenic, and it produces Christians who are nothing like Christ.

Dead to Sin

What shall we say then? Shall we continue in sin, that grace may abound? God forbid. How shall we, that are dead to sin, live any longer therein? Know ye not, that so many of us as were baptized into Jesus Christ were baptized into his death?

Romans 6:1–3

The Apostle Paul powerfully proves in the preceding chapters of Romans that God deals with us by grace through faith, so the logical question he regularly faced was, "*Shall we continue in sin, that grace may abound?*" (Rom. 6:1). Of course, this is not what Paul was saying. He responded by asking, "*How shall we, that are dead to sin, live any longer therein?*" (Rom. 6:2). What a radical statement!

Sadly, the majority of Christians do not believe this today. They believe that they are still alive to sin and that it is with much effort, frustration, and failure that they battle this sin nature the rest of their lives. But that's not what Paul believed. He said that once we are baptized into Christ, we experience a death to our old sin nature. It's dead. It's gone. It doesn't exist anymore. "*Old things are passed away*" (2 Cor. 5:17).

Some of you may be thinking, *Well, I still struggle with many sins, so that means I'm not really dead to sin*. What you may not realize is that this passage in Romans is speaking of your spirit. Your born-again spirit is totally new. It is alive to God, and it is dead to sin. In your new spirit, you are identical to Jesus (1 John 4:17).

I will admit that Christians still sin, and Paul dealt with these things in more detail in Romans 7. But, what you need to know now is that if you are born again, your nature has been changed and sin is no longer coming out of your spirit.

At salvation, your "*old man*" (Rom. 6:6), or sin nature, died. Christians don't have a sin nature that compels them to sin. So why do so many born-again believers still struggle with sin? It's because the tendency to sin remains in the thoughts and emotions—the soul—that the old man left behind. The only reason Christians still sin is because they don't know these truths. It's only the truth you know that sets you free (John 8:32).

Renew Your Mind

And be not conformed to this world: but be ye transformed by the renewing of your mind, that ye may prove what is *that good, and acceptable, and perfect, will of God.*

Romans 12:2

In 2 Corinthians 5:17–18, Paul talks about the spirit that you receive at salvation; not your physical body or your soul. As we've already seen, that's evident, because when you get born again your physical body does not automatically change and become new. A lot of people would like it to be that way, but that's not the way it is. If you were overweight before you got saved, you'll still be overweight after you got saved unless you go on a diet or exercise!

Also, your soul is not automatically changed. If you couldn't do math before you got saved, you won't be able to do math after you got saved. But the soul is subject to change—and the key is in the mind.

Romans 12:2 tells us that we should live differently than unbelievers. Most Christians recognize this, but they seem at a loss as to how to accomplish it. Your mind is part of your soul, so for you to see change in your soul you have to make your thinking line up with God's Word. The Greek word rendered *transformed* is metamorphoo.[5] It's the word from which we derive our English word metamorphosis.

A little caterpillar spins a cocoon and then, after time, turns into a beautiful butterfly. If you want to be transformed from something creepy, crawly, and earthbound into something beautiful that can fly, you need to be metamorphosed or transformed by the renewing of your mind.

If we think on the same things that the world thinks on, we are going to get the same results. If we keep our minds stayed upon God through the study of His Word and fellowship with Him, then we'll have perfect peace (Isaiah 26:3). It's really that simple.

In contrast to the sin nature found in our old spirit, the spirit that we receive at salvation is not a corruptible spirit. It cannot change, but the soul can change. In light of this, once we look at some other scriptures, it will really help you understand what the heart is. It will help you to see that your heart and your spirit are not interchangeable, because your heart is capable of producing some things your spirit is not.

Purify Your Heart

Submit yourselves therefore to God. Resist the devil, and he will flee from you. Draw nigh to God, and he will draw nigh to you. Cleanse your *hands,* ye *sinners; and purify* your *hearts, ye double minded.*

James 4:7–8

The very fact that James tells us to purify our hearts shows that the heart can be impure. However, a born-again spirit cannot be impure. It has already been cleansed and perfected forever (Heb. 10:14).

The born-again spirit you receive at salvation already has the same life, nature, and ability of God in it. What the Apostle Paul says about the fruit of the Spirit (Gal. 5:22-23) is also true of the fruit of the born-again spirit. That spirit produces love, joy, peace, long suffering, gentleness, goodness, faith, meekness, and temperance.

When James says you should purify your heart, he can't be talking about your spirit because your born-again spirit does not need to be purified. Your spirit man is not the part of you that acts in sin anymore. All things in it are of God. But you can still be double-minded in your *heart*.

Your heart can produce envy and strife (James 3:14). Your heart can devise wicked imaginations (Prov. 6:18), meaning your thoughts can be contaminated (2 Cor. 10:4–5). Another thing the heart can do is doubt (Mark 11:23).

Your heart can believe unto righteousness (Rom. 10:10) and it can be slow to believe the things of God (Luke 24:25). Your hearts can reason together with God (Is. 1:18), or against the things of God (Mark 2:8). Your heart can study, be educated, be trained, and be programmed (Prov. 15:28).

Remember, as Jesus is, so are we in this present world (1 John 4:17); not "going to be," but right now. Your born-again spirit is complete. Your spirit doesn't have sin in it, doesn't have worry in it, doesn't have fear in it, and doesn't have any of those other kinds of things.

Your born-again spirit is always thinking the things of God. It has perfect wisdom from God. It has the mind of Christ. It produces the fruit of the Spirit. Once you understand what your born-again spirit produces, and contrast that with some of the other things that come from the heart, then you'll understand that the heart is not solely the spirit—and why it is so important to guard it and purify it!

Have No Fear

For God hath not given us the spirit of fear; but of power, and of love, and of a sound mind.

2 Timothy 1:7

Faith is a product of the spirit. Doubt and fear are the opposite of faith. Your born-again spirit doesn't operate in fear, but your heart can produce it along with doubt (Mark 11:23) and unbelief (Heb. 3:12).

Remember the Y2K scare at the turn of the millennium? It's a long story, but some people predicted that on January 1, 2000, computer systems around the world—and everything tied to them—would crash, causing widespread chaos.[6] Sad to say, many Christians believed it.

Churches were selling six-month supplies of emergency food and generators. They were urging people to move out of the cities. There were many people who proclaimed it would be the beginning of the Tribulation period.

I didn't agree with what was being taught about Y2K for a number of reasons. The primary thing was that the Lord had told me to go on television, and my program wasn't scheduled to broadcast until January 3, 2000. If everything that was predicted to happen actually occurred, then I wouldn't be on television! So, I just felt in my heart that Y2K wouldn't result in disaster. And, wouldn't you know, it turned out to be a nonevent!

The world likes to exaggerate, lie, and present people with the worst-case scenarios because bad news sells. Instead of the nightly news, it's become more like the nightly prophecy! This seemed to be the case during the pandemic a few years ago. People bought into all the bad news and made all sorts of corresponding decisions contrary to the Word of God. Those things didn't come out of a born-again spirit, which doesn't produce fear. They came from something else!

My point is these were Christians—with incorruptible, born-again spirits on the inside of them—who responded out of a sense of fear during the Y2K scare. This fear was ungodly and not a product of the spirit.

You can take many scriptures about the heart and bring them all to bear once you see that the spirit part of you is complete. But if these things are produced by the heart, that means something other than your born-again spirit is at work. So, where do things like doubt, fear, unbelief, and evil imaginations come from?

Inspect Your Fruit

Beloved, now are we the sons of God, and it doth not yet appear what we shall be: but we know that, when he shall appear, we shall be like him; for we shall see him as he is. And every man that hath this hope in him purifieth himself, even as he is pure.

1 John 3:2–3

Every person who's truly born of God and has this hope of seeing Him will seek to purify themselves. Now, they may do a poor job of it because maybe they've never really renewed their minds to the Word of God. Maybe they're still under condemnation. But that desire is there. John verifies this in these verses by saying, "Look, your spirit man's born of God, it doesn't commit sin, and if that spirit is really within you then it's going to start leading you out of sin."

I don't consider myself to be the judge of a person, but I can be a fruit inspector (Matt. 7:16–20). A person's lifestyle and actions yield fruit that tells us a lot about them. If a person is just living openly in sin, you may be very skeptical about whether they're born again. John is saying a person who's actually born of God seeks to purify themselves because the born-again spirit within hates, rebels at, and resists ungodliness.

Your spirit is not the part of you that doubts because it says in 2 Corinthians 5:18 that all things are of God when we are new creations in Christ. Doubt is not of God. Fear is not of God. Unbelief is not of God. The Bible also says that confusion is not of God. In 1 Corinthians 14:33, Paul said, "*God is not the author of confusion*." So, confusion is not a product of the born-again spirit. But these things are all capacities of the mind, which is part of the soul.

You need to renew your mind, but you don't need to renew your born-again spirit. Your spirit has been changed already (2 Cor. 5:17). But it is your soul—the part of you trained by your old sin nature before you were born again—that needs to be renewed.

I believe your soul is part of your heart, which also includes your spirit. You have to get your soul into agreement with your born-again spirit through renewing your mind. Our minds are similar to computers in the sense that they can be programmed. And once programmed, they will continue to function as programmed until we reprogram them.

The Divided Heart

Their heart is divided; now shall they be found faulty: he shall break down their altars, he shall spoil their images.

Hosea 10:2

This is talking about the children of Israel, and how their hearts were divided. That goes along with being double-minded. The heart can be divided, but the spirit man cannot. Everything in the born-again spirit is of God, and God is not the author of confusion (1 Cor. 14:33).

As we've seen, the terms *spirit* and *heart* are not interchangeable. They do not mean exactly the same thing. I believe the spirit is a part of the heart, but it is not the whole thing. The heart of man contains both the spirit and the soul. And yet, there are scriptures where the word *heart* is definitely referring to the spirit. So, what's the answer?

You have to read scriptures in context and determine whether they are speaking about your born-again spirit, or the things that come out of the soul—which includes the mind, will, emotions, and conscience. This will give you more understanding of verses like Deuteronomy 6:5:

And thou shalt love the Lord thy God with all thine heart, and with all thy soul, and with all thy might.

Now, your born-again spirit is already serving God. It's not the part of us that sins. It's not the part of us that gets depressed. It's not the part of us that wants to do things contrary to God. Again, your spirit man is serving God, but you don't just experience that victory automatically. You've got to change your heart by changing your mind.

We were all born in sin, and our old sin nature programmed our minds how to be selfish, bitter, angry, and all those negative things. Your sin nature may be dead and gone once you get born again, but it left behind a carnal mind (Rom. 8:6–7). It will still function as programmed until it is reprogrammed. Our lives are transformed by the renewing of our minds (Rom. 12:2).

You see, as your soul and spirit come into agreement through the renewing of your mind, you will serve God with your whole heart. Once you've done that, your physical body will automatically follow along with whatever your inner person does. I'll explain more about how to renew your mind in the next sections.

The Master Control System

And the Lord God formed man of *the dust of the ground, and breathed into his nostrils the breath of life; and man became a living soul.*

Genesis 2:7

Your soul is really like the master control of your system. Now, God intended the spirit man to give the soul commands, and then the soul would be the part that dominated the physical body. It's the part that would control all the other things. The orders would come from the spirit, but the soul had the capability. The soul has the will to decide what to do with the spirit's commands; whether to submit or rebel.

You cannot just ignore the soul and let the spirit dominate. You can't just take your soul, separate it, and put it somewhere by itself. It's not that way even when a person dies—their spirit does not separate from their soul.

At death, the spirit leaves the body. But we also know from Revelation 6:9, when the fifth seal was opened, John "*saw under the altar the souls of them that were slain for the word of God and for the testimony which they held.*" He saw their souls and not their spirits. That's because the soul and the spirit stay together. When the spirit leaves the body, the soul goes with it. These people, who had their spirits leave their bodies, were seen in heaven with their souls intact.

Their souls were recognizable, and John saw people as their souls. I believe that our souls look just like our physical bodies. The soul has arms, legs, and all those kinds of things. It must resemble us to such a degree that people can recognize our souls as us.

Our soul is our personality part. There will be personalities in heaven. They'll be glorified personalities that no longer have the hang-ups that we do here, but we will still have our personalities.

My point is that the spirit and the soul were meant to function together. I believe that they were imparted into man at the same time—in the heart. One of the things that made the sin in the garden so bad was the fact that the soul and the spirit ceased to function together. The soul began to listen to the input from the physical body instead.

After the fall (Gen. 3:6–7), mankind worked from the outside-in rather than the inside-out. In other words, mankind's sense knowledge began to take over. The lust of their flesh began to dominate them instead of the soul taking its orders from the spirit.

There was a break. There was a breach. And when that happened, their sin was transgression and the spirit within man died. When a person gets born again, they get a new spirit, but they still have that old soul left behind. It is not yet renewed.

We Have the Mind of Christ

For who hath known the mind of the Lord, that he may instruct him? But we have the mind of Christ.

1 Corinthians 2:16

We've already established that your born-again spirit is complete. That means your spirit is not the part of you that's growing and being renewed to God's Word. Now, I know that that goes contrary to a lot of teaching.

A lot of people think that their spirit is like a baby; it's got to be grown, matured, and exercised. No! Your born-again spirit is complete, like a grown man. It is as Christ is (1 John 4:17), and He is not a baby that's growing. He is already complete!

Your born-again spirit already has the mind of Christ. It knows all things. All the wisdom and treasures of God are in Christ Jesus. But your soul is still corrupted with the thoughts and ways you were taught before you got born again. So, the Christian life is all about learning to renew your mind—your soul—to the Word of God so you may be transformed. That's how we draw out those things of God from our born-again spirits.

We sometimes talk about people getting the Word in their heads and not getting it in their hearts. That means you don't just need intellectual knowledge; you need revelation knowledge. You need something from the Word that is a reality to you and not just the ability to quote Bible facts. You need to get the life of God out of His Word and flowing in you.

In reality, you are trying to get the Word into your mind, which isn't in your head; it's in your soul. You are trying to renew your soul to the truth of God's Word. So, you are really trying to get the Word into your heart. Your soul is the part of your heart that needs the Word of God.

When the Bible talks about serving the Lord with your whole heart, that means you can get to the place where your spirit man serves God along with your mind, will, emotions, conscience, mental capacity, and all these things that are part of your soul. That's when you'll truly see God's best operating in your life.

At this point, you may be thinking, *Well, how do I know which is which inside my own heart?*

Sharper Than a Two-Edged Sword

For the word of God is quick, and powerful, and sharper than any twoedged sword, piercing even to the dividing asunder of soul and spirit, and of the joints and marrow, and is a discerner of the thoughts and intents of the heart.

Hebrews 4:12

This is talking about how sharp the Word of God is. It's sharp enough to divide the soul and spirit. Now, I do not believe you can just take the spirit and separate it from the soul. They were imparted to us by God, and they were meant to function as one unit. That's not what this is talking about. But you really begin to gain victory in the Christian life when you can believe God with your whole heart—spirit and soul combined as one unit.

What this scripture is talking about is the "*dividing asunder of soul and spirit*," and the only thing that can do it is the Word of God. It is what you use to discern whether something is coming to you out of your born-again spirit man or out of your soul.

Your born-again spirit will never produce anything contrary to God's Word. If you consider something that is against God's Word, it came out of the soul which is still programmed according to your old, dead sin nature—from your unrenewed mind. If that's the case, it needs to be cast down and brought into subjection to God's Word (2 Cor. 10:4-5).

If a thought comes out of your born-again spirit, that's the voice of the Holy Spirit speaking through your spirit, and you need to learn to respond to it. The Word of God is "a *discerner of the thoughts and intents of the heart*" (Heb. 4:12).

The Bible likens the spirit and soul to the marrow and joints of the bone. The marrow is in the hollow center of your bones. This is where your body produces the life that is in the blood. The Bible says the life of the physical body is in your blood (Lev. 17:11). So, you could say that the marrow represents the life-giving part of your body. Well, that's what the spirit is.

The joint would represent the soul. Joints join different parts of the body together. In other words, a joint would connect one bone to another bone; it goes between them. And that's what the soul does. The soul takes spiritual directives and transfers them into physical realities. The physical body responds directly to the soul. So, the soul is the joint between the spirit and the physical realm.

The spirit and the soul function together, and the Word of God is a discerner of the thoughts and the intents of the heart. "Thoughts" refers to the soul, while "intents of the heart" refers to the spirit. The spirit is where your intents—your desires—arise from. Your thoughts come out of your mental capabilities. You realize victory when you get your thoughts in line with your intents. Praise God!

Put the Word in Your Heart

Then said Jesus to those Jews which believed on him, If ye continue in my word, then *are ye my disciples indeed; and ye shall know the truth, and the truth shall make you free.*

John 8:31–32

I believe America is at a tipping point. We are divided. And this division isn't based on whether someone is a Republican or a Democrat, or even a conservative or a liberal. It's a battle between good and evil; light and darkness.

If you look at political polls, you'll notice how people will look at the same issue and, based on what they believe, come to completely different conclusions about it. Whether it's abortion, homosexuality, transgenderism, socialism, or anything else, how someone views the world will determine how they view these issues.

It all really comes down to discipleship. By Jesus' own definition, a disciple is a person who continues in His Word until they are set free by the truth. The church has not emphasized God's Word nearly enough, and it's caused millions of people who claim to be Christians to not live according to what the Bible has to say. Their hearts are not being changed by God's Word. So, they are not discerning these issues biblically.

Several years ago, I had a Charis student tell me that the school radically changed her life. She said she was extremely liberal on social issues when she first came, but by graduation, she had become so conservative that many in her own family had nearly disowned her because of her beliefs.

I asked this woman to explain how she had been able to say she loved the Lord, and yet also had supported abortion, homosexuality, transgenderism, and other ungodly things. She said, "I loved God, but I didn't love the Bible. When I came to Charis, I learned to love the Word of God, and that changed everything. You can't love God's Word and be a liberal."

This is why it is important to renew the mind—reprogram your soul—to act in line with your born-again spirit. People who draw out the things of God from their born-again spirits will be able to see things the way He does and respond accordingly. But unless you become a disciple, you will continue living just like your unsaved neighbors.

The Word of God contains total power (Ps. 128:2 and Heb. 1:3), but it has to be planted in our hearts and allowed to germinate before it releases that power. The one thing I've done is to take God's Word and let it produce miraculous results for me and through me. My whole life and ministry are the product of meditating on God's Word. Any good thing in my life or ministry can be traced back to how God's Word has changed me. I believe it can be the same for you.

The Heart Has to Change

This *I say then, Walk in the Spirit, and ye shall not fulfil the lust of the flesh. For the flesh lusteth against the Spirit, and the Spirit against the flesh: and these are contrary the one to the other: so that ye cannot do the things that ye would.*

Galatians 5:16–17

The problem isn't out there. The problem isn't your lack of education, the color of your skin, your lack of finances, or your situation at home. Some of those things may aggravate what's already on the inside of you, but it goes much deeper than anything that the world has to offer. You've got to go to the root of the problem, which is a person's heart. And their heart has to change.

At the time of this writing, the prison recidivism rate in the United States shows that all the government programs, psychology, and other worldly solutions are just not working. According to the Department of Justice, nearly half of all federal prisoners are arrested again within eight years of their release. At the state level, it's even worse; around 80 percent are arrested again over that same time period.[7] That's just terrible!

Years ago, when Jamie and I were ministering in England, we visited a place that had been a prison centuries ago. Back then, when a person was arrested, they were thrown into this prison. Not only were they confined, but they had to pay to be lodged and fed. In many cases, these people ran up debts so steep they could never get out.

In the early years of the United States, it was the Christians who stepped in to reform the penal system.

Before that time, if someone committed a crime, they would be beaten, put in the stocks, or be executed. Eventually believers offered to preach the Gospel to criminals while they were locked away. These people would get born again, their hearts would change, they would be released, and they would become contributing members of society. This is why it came to be called the "correction system."

Sadly, at some point, the government took over, the Gospel wasn't preached any more, and people's hearts weren't being changed. It's gotten to be that, if a person wasn't a career criminal when they went into prison, they are by the time they get out! People don't need more psychology or government programs. The solution to a problem isn't throwing money at it or developing a social program to let the government address it. People need the Gospel if they're ever going to see their hearts changed.

Love God with Your Whole Heart

And thou shalt love the Lord thy God with all thy heart, and with all thy soul, and with all thy mind, and with all thy strength: this is the first commandment.

Mark 12:30

Years ago, a friend of mine got born again in the mental ward of a hospital. He was in there because the doctors said he had lost his mind. He didn't know who he was, where he was coming from, or where he was going. Because he had such a severe break, he didn't really have an identity.

This man grew up in abject poverty. He didn't go to school on a regular basis because his parents were both alcoholics. As a matter of fact, he'd sometimes go months without any clothes, just running around in his underwear until the welfare people would come get him. They would give him some second-hand clothes, and he'd go to school for a little while, wearing those clothes until they wore out. Then, he'd just stay at home again.

He had a terrible childhood. And when he grew up, he fried his brain on drugs, ran into trouble with the police, and was just a mess. But when he got born again in that mental ward, he was like a blank slate. When this man was given a Bible, he really didn't know who he was. So, he read about Jesus in the Word—and decided to be just like Him!

When we first met this man, he was so kind and generous to us that I leaned over to Jamie and said, "I'm going to keep my hand on my wallet!" In my experience, it was just so unusual that someone would be that nice without some other motivation. But this man had totally renewed his mind to the Word of God—and he was living like Jesus.

You see, this man's old sin nature was gone. He was born again—a new creature. His spirit was complete and all things in it were of God. And he renewed his mind to the Word of God, which totally transformed him from someone who lived in poverty, used drugs, and broke the law, into someone new.

For example, when people wanted something from him, he just asked himself, "What would Jesus do?" And he imitated Jesus! He became the pastor of a church with thousands of people and personally gave tens of thousands of dollars every month. He's one of the most godly people I've ever known, all because he renewed his mind to the Word, decided to be like Jesus, and served God with his whole heart! That's awesome!

Conclusion

Brothers and sisters, if we would just understand the heart, it would clear up so much confusion over how to live the Christian life. The truth is your born-again spirit is complete. It is full of the things of God.

Once you start sowing the incorruptible seed of the Word of God (1 Pet. 1:23) into your heart, the soulish part of your heart will start working together with your born-again spirit to serve God wholly (1 Thess. 5:23). I'll tell you, sometimes things are so simple you need help to misunderstand them.

If you want to see change outwardly, it has to begin on the inside by sowing the Word of God. If you can just change the way you think—the way you are on the inside— then you'll see change happen in your life effortlessly! But it all starts with your heart. As you begin to understand this, it will really help you in that pursuit.

I hope this booklet has helped you see that the heart is not simply the spirit. The heart is the combination of spirit and soul. As you understand this, you'll be able to start serving God with your whole heart.

FURTHER STUDY

If you enjoyed this booklet and would like to learn more about some of the things I've shared, I suggest my teachings:

1. *Spirit, Soul & Body*
2. *Hardness of Heart*
3. *How to Prepare Your Heart*
4. *The New You & The Holy Spirit*
5. *Effortless Change*
6. *The Old Man is Dead*

These teachings are available for free at **awmi.net**, or they can be purchased at **awmi.net/store**.

Receive Jesus as Your Savior

Choosing to receive Jesus Christ as your Lord and Savior is the most important decision you'll ever make!

God's Word promises, *"That if thou shalt confess with thy mouth the Lord Jesus, and shalt believe in thine heart that God hath raised him from the dead, thou shalt be saved. For with the heart man believeth unto righteousness; and with the mouth confession is made unto salvation"* (Rom. 10:9–10). *"For whosoever shall call upon the name of the Lord shall be saved"* (Rom. 10:13). By His grace, God has already done everything to provide salvation. Your part is simply to believe and receive.

Pray out loud: "Jesus, I acknowledge that I've sinned and need to receive what you did for the forgiveness of my sins. I confess that You are my Lord and Savior. I believe in my heart that God raised You from the dead. By faith in Your Word, I receive salvation now. Thank You for saving me."

The very moment you commit your life to Jesus Christ, the truth of His Word instantly comes to pass in your spirit. Now that you're born again, there's a brand-new you!

Please contact us and let us know that you've prayed to receive Jesus as your Savior. We'd like to send you some free materials to help you on your new journey. Call our Helpline: **719-635-1111** (available 24 hours a day, seven days a week) to speak to a staff member who is here to help you understand and grow in your new relationship with the Lord.

Welcome to your new life!

Receive the Holy Spirit

As His child, your loving heavenly Father wants to give you the supernatural power you need to live a new life. *"For every one that asketh receiveth; and he that seeketh findeth; and to him that knocketh it shall be opened…how much more shall* your *heavenly Father give the Holy Spirit to them that ask him?"* (Luke 11:10–13).

All you have to do is ask, believe, and receive! Pray this: "Father, I recognize my need for Your power to live a new life. Please fill me with Your Holy Spirit. By faith, I receive it right now. Thank You for baptizing me. Holy Spirit, You are welcome in my life."

Some syllables from a language you don't recognize will rise up from your heart to your mouth (1 Cor. 14:14). As you speak them out loud by faith, you're releasing God's power from within and building yourself up in the spirit (1 Cor. 14:4). You can do this whenever and wherever you like.

It doesn't really matter whether you felt anything or not when you prayed to receive the Lord and His Spirit. If you believed in your heart that you received, then God's Word promises you did. *"Therefore I say unto you, What things soever ye desire, when ye pray, believe that ye receive* them, *and ye shall have* them" (Mark 11:24). God always honors His Word—believe it!

We would like to rejoice with you, pray with you, and answer any questions to help you understand more fully what has taken place in your life!

Please contact us to let us know that you've prayed to be filled with the Holy Spirit and to request the book *The New You & the Holy Spirit.* This book will explain in more detail about the benefits of being filled with the Holy Spirit and speaking in tongues. Call our Helpline: **719-635-1111** (available 24 hours a day, seven days a week).

Endnotes

1. *Blue Letter Bible*, s.v. "heart." Accessed October 10, 2023, https://www.blueletterbible.org/search/search. cfm?Criteria=heart&t=KJV#s=s_primary_0_1

2. "Survey: Majority of Americans No Longer See Human Life as 'Sacred,' Yet See Humanity as 'Basically Good,'" Cultural Resource. Accessed June 23, 2020, https://www.arizonachristian.edu/wp-content/ uploads/2020/06/AWVI-2020-Release-07-Perceptions- of-Value-of-Life.pdf

3. *Founders Online*, "Letter from John Adams to Massachusetts Militia, 11 October 1798," National Historical Publications and Records Commission, the National Archives. Accessed November 24, 2023, https://founders.archives.gov/documents/ Adams/99-02-02-3102

4. John Wesley, Wesley's Notes on the Bible, Wesley Center Online, accessed October 10, 2023, https:// www.ccel.org/ccel/wesley/notes.ii.xx.lii.ii.html

5. *Blue Letter Bible*, s.v. "μεταμορφόω" ("metamorphoō"). Accessed August 18, 2023, https://www.blueletterbible. org/lexicon/g3339/kjv/tr/0-1/

6. "Y2K," National Museum of American History, accessed October 27, 2023, https://americanhistory.si.edu/collections/object-groups/y2k

7. "A Second Chance: The Impact of Unsuccessful Reentry and the Need for Reintegration Resources in Communities," *Community Policing Dispatch*, April 2022, https://cops.usdoj.gov/html/dispatch/04-2022/reintegration_resources.html

Call for Prayer

If you need prayer for any reason, you can call our Helpline, 24 hours a day, seven days a week at **719-635-1111**. A trained prayer minister will answer your call and pray with you.

Every day, we receive testimonies of healings and other miracles from our Helpline, and we are ministering God's nearly-too-good-to-be-true message of the Gospel to more people than ever. So, I encourage you to call today!

About the Author

Andrew Wommack's life was forever changed the moment he encountered the supernatural love of God on March 23, 1968. As a renowned Bible teacher and author, Andrew has made it his mission to change the way the world sees God.

Andrew's vision is to go as far and deep with the Gospel as possible. His message goes far through the *Gospel Truth* television program, which is available to over half the world's population. The message goes deep through discipleship at Charis Bible College, headquartered in Woodland Park, Colorado. Founded in 1994, Charis has campuses across the United States and around the globe.

Andrew also has an extensive library of teaching materials in print, audio, and video. More than 200,000 hours of free teachings can be accessed at **awmi.net**.

Contact Information

Andrew Wommack Ministries, Inc.

PO Box 3333
Colorado Springs, CO 80934-3333
info@awmi.net
awmi.net

Helpline: 719-635-1111 (available 24/7)

Charis Bible College

info@charisbiblecollege.org
844-360-9577
CharisBibleCollege.org

For a complete list of all of our offices,
visit **awmi.net/contact-us**.

Connect with us on social media.

There's more on the website!

Discover **FREE** teachings, testimonies, and more by scanning the QR code or visiting **awmi.net**.

Continue to grow in the Word of God!
You will be blessed!

ANDREW WOMMACK MINISTRIES

Your monthly giving makes the greatest kingdom impact

When you give, you make an impact in the kingdom that lasts for generations. Your generosity enables our phone ministers to answer calls 24/7. Your support is also expanding Charis Bible College and allowing *The Gospel Truth* to reach an even wider global audience. You do this and more through your giving each month!

Become a Grace Partner today! Scan the QR code, visit **awmi.net/partner** or call our Helpline at **719-635-1111** and select option five for Partnership

Andrew's

LIVING
COMMENTARY
BIBLE SOFTWARE

Andrew Wommack's *Living Commentary* Bible study software is a user-friendly, downloadable program. It's like reading the Bible with Andrew at your side, sharing his revelation with you verse by verse.

Main features:

- Bible study software with a grace-and-faith perspective
- Over 26,000 notes by Andrew on verses from Genesis through Revelation
- *Matthew Henry's Concise Commentary*
- 12 Bible versions
- 2 concordances: *Englishman's Concordance* and *Strong's Concordance*
- 2 dictionaries: *Collaborative International Dictionary* and *Holman's Dictionary*
- Atlas with biblical maps
- Bible and *Living Commentary* statistics
- Quick navigation, including history of verses
- Robust search capabilities (for the Bible and Andrew's notes)
- "Living" (i.e., constantly updated and expanding)
- Ability to create personal notes

Whether you're new to studying the Bible or a seasoned Bible scholar, you'll gain a deeper revelation of the Word from a grace-and-faith perspective.

Purchase Andrew's *Living Commentary* today at **awmi.net/living**, and grow in the Word with Andrew.

Item code: 8350

ANDREW
WOMMACK
MINISTRIES

www.ingramcontent.com/pod-product-compliance
Lightning Source LLC
Chambersburg PA
CBHW071638040426
42452CB00009B/1679